THE FIRST LOVE COOKIE CLUB COOKBOOK

FROM TWILIGHT, TEXAS

LORI WILDE

CHRISTIE CONLEE

CONTENTS

WELCOME TO THE FIRST LOVE COOKIE CLUB'S CHRISTMAS COOKBOOK

This Christmas cookie cookbook has been lovingly created for you by the quaint and kooky denizens of Twilight, Texas.

In the following pages, you'll find the "rules" for Cookie Club and a baker's dozen of our most delicious Christmas cookie recipes.

We're confident you'll discover a recipe destined to become one of your Christmas favorites.

From our hearts to yours! We wish for you the very merriest of Christmases and a joyous holiday season.

If you would like to read the books on which the town of Twilight, Texas is based, you can order them from Lori Wilde's website @ www.loriwilde.com

RULES OF THE FIRST LOVE COOKIE
CLUB

****

Rule #1

Women only. No men. No kids. This club is for mothers, daughters, sisters, and female friends. We let our hair down, drink a little wine, talk a little trash, and try out some interesting cookie recipes. Kids and men just get in the way.

Rule #2

All the cookies must be homemade. No store-bought cookies allowed. Period. End of Story.

Rule #3

Whatever happens, or is said, at Cookie Club, stays at Cookie Club.

Rule #4

No chocolate chip cookies allowed. Chocolate chips are not Christmas cookies, no matter how tasty. You may use chocolate chips in another recipe, but no straight-up chocolate chip cookies.

Rule #5

Festive holiday attire is to be worn to the meeting. Ugly Christmas sweaters are not only encouraged but fully embraced. Show off your Christmas kitsch.

PEPPERMINT HOT CHOCOLATE COOKIES

Peppermint
Hot Chocolate
COOKIES

SUBMITTED BY
Dotty Mae Densmore

Submitted by Dotty Mae Densmore, who loves all things peppermint, particularly peppermint schnapps, these cookies are magically delicious. If you're the sort to imbibe, have a tipple of peppermint schnapps while baking these mouthwatering cookies. According to Dotty Mae, it makes things oh, so merry and bright.

INGREDIENTS

- 1 cup softened butter
- 3/4 cup granulated sugar
- 2/3 cup packed brown sugar
- 2 large eggs
- 1 tablespoon peppermint extract
- 3 ½ cups flour
- 3/4 cup hot cocoa mix (about 5 packets)
- 1 teaspoon salt
- 1 ½ teaspoons baking soda
- 1 cup chocolate chips (dark or semi-sweet)
- Vanilla buttercream icing (Dotty Mae uses store-bought, but you can make your own.)
- Crushed peppermint candies for garnish

Instructions

Before she gets started in on the schnapps, Dotty Mae likes to preheat her oven to 350°. (So that she doesn't forget once the schnapps kicks in. Dotty Mae *is* over eighty, y'all.) She also likes to line the baking sheets with parchment paper to make cleanup a breeze.

She gets out a medium-sized mixing bowl, and sifts the dry ingredients together (flour, salt, baking soda, hot chocolate mix) She's had this set of mixing bowls since forever. She bought them from Montgomery Wards (affectionately called Monkey Wards by her two boys) when she worked there as a manager.

With a mixer, beat butter and sugars until light and fluffy. Sometimes, if Dotty Mae has had more than a jigger of schnapps, she'll put Michael Jackson on the record player and sing "Beat It" at the top of her lungs. It's a hoot.

Add eggs one at a time and beat well after each addition. Then add mint extract and mix to incorporate. Or, if you're like Dotty Mae, go ahead and toss in a splash of peppermint schnapps.

On low, slowly incorporate dry ingredients. Do not overbeat. Dotty Mae suggests turning off "Beat It" at this point least you get carried away with the beating.

Stir in chocolate chips and marshmallows with a spatula.

Use a teaspoon-sized cookie scoop and place cookies evenly on baking sheet.

Bake 10 to 12 minutes. Remove from oven and cool completely.

When cooled, spread icing on top of the cookie and garnish with crushed peppermint candies.

Servings—50 cookies

Pour yourself another shot of peppermint schnapps and toast yourself. You've done a great job!

KISMET COOKIES

Kismet Cookies

*Sleep with a kismet cookie under your pillow
on Christmas Eve and dream of your one true
love*

SUBMITTED BY SARAH COLLIER'S GRANDMOTHER,
MIA

*Y*ou've heard the hullabaloo about these cookies, but in case you're new in town, here's the scoop...

Bake this recipe on Christmas Eve. Slip a kismet cookie underneath your pillow before you go to sleep, and you will dream of your one true love.

This recipe was handed down to Sarah Collier Walker from her Gramma Mia. One year, on Christmas Eve, Sarah followed the instructions and dreamed of her one true love, but it kind of blew up in her face. If you want to know how that turned out, you'll need to read Sarah's story in *The First Love Cookie Club*.

P.S. The dream thing works *only* on Christmas Eve.

INGREDIENTS

- 3/4 cup all-purpose flour
- 3/4 teaspoon salt
- 1/2 teaspoon baking soda
- 1 teaspoon ground cinnamon
- 3/4 cup butter, softened
- 3/4 cup granulated sugar
- 3/4 cup packed light brown sugar
- 1 egg
- 1 tablespoon water
- 1 tablespoon vanilla, divided
- 3 cups uncooked quick or old-fashioned oats
- 3/4 cup cranberries
- 1 cup macadamia nuts, chopped
- 1/2 cup white chocolate chunks, chopped

Instructions

Each year, Sarah and her grandmother would make these cookies together. Gramma Mia would trot out the flour and sugar and vanilla and creamy, honest-to-goodness butter (which Sarah's mom wouldn't let her eat) and assemble the ingredients on the shiny white tiles of her kitchen counter.

They would preheat the oven to 375°, and lines their baking sheets with parchment paper.

In a small bowl, Sarah would stir together flour, salt, baking soda, and cinnamon.

While Gramma Mia would man the large mixing bowl with an electric mixer on medium speed, beat butter, granulated sugar, and brown sugar until light and fluffy.

Then she would add the egg, water, and 2 teaspoons vanilla and mix well.

With the mixer on low speed, Gramma Mia would gradually add the dry flour mixture and beat just until blended.

Sarah loved to stir in oats and then add in the cranberries, macadamia nuts, and white chocolate chunks.

Taking turns, they would drop dough by a tablespoon about 2 inches apart, onto the parchment-prepared baking sheets.

Sarah would watch through the window of the stove as the cookies baked until the edges were golden brown, about 9 to 10 minutes.

Gramma Mia removed them from the oven and let cookies cool on the sheets for 2 minutes. Sarah hated this part because she wanted to gobble them up right away. Then her grandmother would transfer the cookies to wire racks to cool completely.

At last, they would sit at the kitchen table with a glass of milk and eat cookies until it was time for bed.

After putting out cookies for Santa, Sarah would put a cookie in a plastic baggie so she wouldn't get crumbs on Gramma Mia's bedding, crawl into bed and dream of her one true love.

Happily, these cookies can be stored in an airtight container and frozen for up to 3 months.

Servings—32 cookies

PEANUT BUTTER SPRITZ COOKIES

Peanut Butter Spritz Cookies

THE FIRST LOVE COOKIE CLUB
Submitted by Terri Longoria

$\mathcal{T}$erri Longoria, the owner of Hot Legs Gym and Day Spa, submitted these yummy cookies. If she's going to cheat on her diet, you can bet she'll make sure her temptations have plenty of protein to balance out those pesky carbs. She's got the best legs in town, so she's obviously doing something right.

These cookies make a great on-the-go breakfast treat.

INGREDIENTS

- 1/2 cup butter, softened
- 1/2 cup creamy peanut butter
- 1/2 cup granulated sugar
- 1/2 cup packed light brown sugar
- 1 large egg
- 1 teaspoon vanilla extract
- 1 ½ cups all-purpose flour
- 3/4 teaspoon baking soda
- 1/2 teaspoon baking powder
- 1/4 teaspoon salt
- Chocolate chips, melted (dark or semi-sweet)
- 1 cup finely chopped unsalted peanuts

Instructions

Terri likes to bake early in the day so she can have all day to burn off those calories. After her three-mile morning run, she preheats her oven to 350° and lines a baking sheet with parchment paper.

In a large bowl—she loves using the Fiestaware mixing bowl her mother-in-law got her for Christmas last year—she creams the butter, peanut butter, and sugars until it is light and fluffy. Then she beats in the egg and vanilla.

While she's combining the flour, baking soda, baking powder, and salt; and gradually adding into the creamed mixture and mixing well, she does deep breathing exercises. You don't have to do this when you're making the cookies, but deep breathing keeps Terri chill.

Then she covers the dough and refrigerates it for 30 minutes or until easy to handle. Terri spends time doing yoga.

She recommends using a cookie press that is fitted with a star disk that she found at a cute little cooking store on the Twilight town square, Terri presses dough 2 inches apart into oblong strips on baking sheets. Then she cuts each strip into 2-inch pieces (do not separate pieces).

Bake until golden brown, 7 to 9 minutes. Terri turns on Christmas music and dances around the kitchen while she waits. After the cookies are done, she removes them to wire racks to cool.

When the cookies are cooled, she melts chocolate chips in the microwave; stirring until smooth. She dips one end of each cookie into chocolate; allows the excess to drip off. Coats with peanuts. Places on waxed paper; and lets it stand until set.

She enjoys the cookie she's earned through all that exercise with a cup of hot black coffee.

RED VELVET THUMBPRINT COOKIES

Red Velvet Thumbprint Cookies

SUBMITTED BY PATSY CROUCH

*T*hese rich cookies were submitted by Sheriff Hondo's lovely bride, Patsy Calloway Cross Crouch. It took these two former high school sweethearts forty years to find their way back to each other, but the wait was worth it. Hondo says these cookies played an instrumental role in their romance, but if you push for details, he just grins like a Cheshire cat and clams right up.

Let's just say these cookies are the stuff of dreams and leave it at that.

INGREDIENTS

- 1 cup butter, softened
- 1 cup granulated sugar
- 1 large egg
- 2 to 4 teaspoons red food coloring
- 2 ½ cups all-purpose flour
- 3 tablespoons baking cocoa
- 1 teaspoon instant espresso powder
- 1 teaspoon baking powder
- 1/4 teaspoon salt
- Chocolate chips, melted (dark or semi-sweet)
- 1/2 cup Andes mints, chopped

Instructions

Patsy says to make sure and preheat your oven to 350° and to line the baking sheets with parchment paper.

Hondo pulls the shades so no one can peek inside the house and he dons one of Patsy's frilly aprons and helps out. (She sells the aprons at her boutique shop, The Teal Peacock, and they are adorable.) Patsy uses a large bowl, to cream butter and sugar until light and fluffy, and then beats in egg and food coloring.

Meanwhile, Hondo is busy whisking together the dry ingredients. Flour, cocoa, instant espresso powder, baking powder, and salt. Hondo passes them off to Patsy who gradually beats the ingredients into the creamed mixture.

While Patsy shapes dough into 1-inch balls and places them 1 inch apart on the ungreased baking sheets lined with parchment paper, Hondo makes a deep indentation in the center of each ball with his thumb.

She pops them in the oven to bake 8 to 9 minutes or until set. Hondo washes up while Patsy removes the cookies from the pans to wire racks to cool completely.

*Note: If thumb indentation did not set during baking—but they usually do because Hondo has such a firm touch—press in the center of cookies while warm.

In a microwave, Patsy melts chocolate chips; and stirs until smooth. Then Hondo spoons a scant teaspoon filling into each cookie. Drizzles the tops with remaining mixture and sprinkles them with Andes candies.

Servings—30 cookies

Hondo and Patsy take a plateful to the bedroom, and we'll let your imagination fill in the rest. They do have forty years to make up for after all…

GLAZED SOFT SPICE COOKIES

FIRST LOVE COOKIE CLUB

GLAZED SOFT SPICE COOKIES

Elegant, light, delicious

SUBMITTED BY MARVA BULLOCK

*H*igh school principal, Marva Bullock, might be hard-nosed when it comes to running Twilight High, but she's a softy where cookies are concerned. These soft glazed cookies have just the right amount of spice.

INGREDIENTS

For the cookies:
- 4 cups unbleached all-purpose flour
- 1 tablespoon baking powder
- 2 teaspoons cinnamon
- 1/2 teaspoon nutmeg
- 1/2 teaspoon ground cloves
- 1/2 teaspoon salt
- 1/2 cup cold sour cream
- 1/2 cup cold milk
- 1 cup (2 sticks) unsalted butter, softened
- 2 cups packed brown sugar
- 2 large eggs

For the glaze:
- 1/2 cup powdered sugar
- 3 to 4 teaspoons milk

Instructions

Marva is a pretty precision kind of gal, so she keeps the recipe right in front of her as she bakes, even though she's made these cookies hundreds of times.

Stir the flour, baking powder, spices, and salt together in a medium sized mixing bowl. Blend with a whisk and then put aside.

In a small bowl stir the sour cream and milk together with a whisk until well blended and set aside.

In a large bowl beat the butter and sugar together with an electric mixer on medium-high speed until really light and fluffy. (This should take about 4 to 5 minutes.) Scrape down the sides of the bowl with a rubber spatula to ensure everything is well blended.

Beat the eggs in one at a time with the mixer on low speed.

Add the sour cream mixture (Marva says in a pinch you can substitute Greek yogurt) and beat on low speed until well blended, scraping down the sides of the bowl as necessary.

Gradually stir in the flour mixture, just until incorporated.

Cover the dough with plastic wrap and refrigerate it until chilled, at least one hour.

When you are ready to bake the cookies, position one of your oven racks in the center of the oven and preheat your oven to 350°. Line your baking sheets with parchment paper.

Using a teaspoon-sized cookie scoop, drop the cookie dough onto the prepared baking sheets about 2 inches apart. Bake the cookies on the center rack of the oven for 10 to 12 minutes, or until the cookies are puffed, light golden brown, and no longer look wet.

Remove the baking sheet from the oven and place on a wire rack for 1 to 2 minutes until the cookies cool slightly then transfer the cookies with a metal spatula to the wire racks to cool completely. (They will fall a little as they cool.)

Once the cookies have cooled, in a small bowl combine milk and powdered sugar with a whisk until smooth. Dip cookies into the glaze to ice the top of each cookie.

Once the icing is dry, store the cookies in an airtight container, separating each layer with wax paper so they don't stick together.

Servings—54 cookies

Marva enjoys her cookies with a cup of Earl Grey tea but says hot chai latte pairs nicely too.

ORANGE CHOCOLATE SLICE COOKIES

ORANGE CHOCOLATE SLICE COOKIES

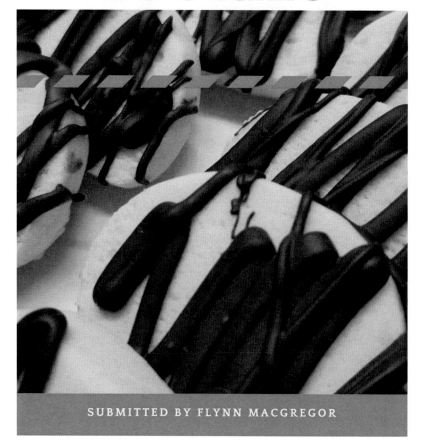

SUBMITTED BY FLYNN MACGREGOR

*S*ubmitted by Flynn MacGregor before she married her high school sweetheart, Jesse Calloway, and became Flynn MacGregor Calloway.

These shortbread cookies pay homage to Flynn's Scottish heritage. She keeps trying to get Jesse to wear a kilt in her family tartan, and serve these at Christmas parties, but Jesse remains firmly defiant. He will do anything for his beloved "Freckles" except wear a "skirt."

INGREDIENTS
- 3/4 cup unsalted butter, softened
- 3/4 cup powdered sugar
- 1 large egg, room temperature
- 2 tablespoons orange juice
- 2 cups + 2 tablespoons all-purpose flour
- 1 tablespoon orange zest
- 1/4 teaspoon salt
- 10 oz. dark chocolate

Instructions

These days Flynn's little ones, Grace and Ian, insist on helping. Using a handheld or stand mixer fitted with the paddle attachment, she beats the butter and powdered sugar until smooth and creamy. She then adds the egg, and orange juice, and beats until combined.

She adds the flour, orange zest, and salt, and beats until combined. If the dough is too sticky to handle, she adds a little flour.

Flynn hands the beaters over to the kids to lick, while she turns the dough out onto a lightly floured surface and shapes it into a 12-inch long log or two 6-inch logs. Flynn says to tightly wrap the log in cling wrap and refrigerate for at least 4 hours, and up to 5 days. (She likes to chill hers overnight.)

When ready to bake, Flynn preheats the oven to 350° and lines a baking tray with parchment paper, or she uses a silicone mat depending on if she can find the mat or not. Ian has a habit of using it for a toy car track.

She slices the log into thick slices and places them onto the prepared baking tray. Bake for 10 to 12 minutes until lightly brown around the edges. Allow cooling for 5 minutes before transferring them to a wire rack to cool completely.

She adds the chocolate to a microwave-safe bowl, and heats in 20-second intervals, stirring after each one, until melted and smooth.

Flynn drizzles each cooled cookie with the melted chocolate and leaves them to set on a baking tray lined with parchment paper. You can refrigerate to set the chocolate quicker.

Servings—24 cookies

Notes:

Cookies stay fresh, in an airtight container, at room temperature or in the fridge for up to 1 week. They also freeze well for up to 3 months. Thaw overnight in the refrigerator before slicing and baking.

But to tell the truth, these cookies don't last that long in the Calloway household. Ian and Grace recommend pairing cookies with ice-cold chocolate milk.

BROWN SUGAR PECAN COOKIES

Brown Sugar Pecan Cookies

SUBMITTED BY EMMA CHEEK

*J*f pralines were cookies, they would be this excellent recipe from our very own Hollywood star, Emma Cheek, owner of the Twilight Playhouse. Each year, Emma and company put on Christmas plays and these cookies are always a welcome addition to the after party.

So break out the spotlight, you're going to want these cookies to take center stage at *your* cookie swap.

INGREDIENTS

- 1 ¼ cup all-purpose flour
- 1/4 teaspoon baking soda
- 1/8 teaspoon salt
- 1/2 cup butter or margarine, softened
- 1 ¼ cup packed brown sugar
- 1 large egg
- 1 cup coarsely chopped pecans

Instructions

Like any good actor, Emma knows the importance of positioning. To that end, when making these cookies, she positions an oven rack center stage—meaning smack dab in the middle of the oven. And she preheats it to 350°.

Depending on your preference, either line baking sheets with parchment paper, or alternatively, lightly grease the cookie sheets. Baker's choice. Although Emma goes with parchment for ease of client.

In a small bowl, whisk together the flour, baking soda, and salt until well blended.

In a large mixing bowl, beat the butter and sugar together with an electric mixer on medium speed until light and fluffy.

Add egg and beat until well blended. Stir in the flour mixture just until blended.

Then stir in the pecans just until distributed through the dough.

Drop by 1/4 teaspoonful about 2 inches apart on the prepared baking sheet.

Bake, one cookie sheet at a time, until golden and set about 7 to 8 minutes. (The cookies will flatten and spread as they bake.)

Remove from the oven and allow to cool for 1 minute on the baking sheet and then transfer the cookies to a wire rack to cool completely.

Make sure your cookie sheet is cold before putting your next batch of dough on it.

Servings—16 cookies

When you serve these cookies, there will be much applause from your audience. Fabulous performance. Now take a bow.

VANILLA BUTTER SUGAR COOKIES

Vanilla Butter Sugar Cookies

SUBMITTED BY
Caitlyn Marsh

*N*othing says Christmas like sugar cookies, and this is a humdinger of a recipe.

Submitted by Caitlyn Marsh Garza, our local florist. When Caitlyn and her husband, former Green Beret, Gideon, entertain they make sure to have lots of beautiful flowers in the house.

Caitlyn says a flowering vanilla orchid makes an excellent accompaniment for these vanilla butter sugar cookies.

INGREDIENTS

- 1 ½ cups butter, softened
- 1 ½ cups granulated sugar
- 2 large eggs
- 2 tablespoons vanilla extract
- 4 cups all-purpose flour
- 1 teaspoon salt
- 1 teaspoon baking soda
- 1 teaspoon cream of tartar

For the frosting:
- 2 sticks unsalted butter, softened
- 3 cups powdered sugar
- 2 to 3 teaspoons milk
- 3 teaspoons vanilla extract

Instructions

Cream butter and granulated sugar until light and fluffy. Beat in eggs and vanilla. In another bowl, whisk flour, salt, baking soda, and cream of tartar. Gradually beat into creamed mixture. Refrigerate, covered, for 30 minutes.

Preheat oven to 350°. On a lightly floured surface, roll dough to 1/4-inch thickness. Cut with floured holiday-related cookie cutters. Place 1 inch apart on ungreased baking sheets. Bake 9 to 11 minutes. Cool on wire racks.

For frosting, beat together butter and powdered sugar until well blended and smooth. Increase mixer speed and continue beating for another 3 minutes. Pour in vanilla extract and continue beating until combined. Add 2 teaspoons milk and continue beating.

If you feel the consistency is still too thick, add one more teaspoon of milk and beat again. If desired, add a few drops of food coloring. Cut a small hole in the tip of a pastry bag or in the corner of a food-safe plastic bag; transfer frosting to bag. Pipe decorations. Sprinkle with colored sugar.

Freeze option: Freeze undecorated cookies, layered between waxed paper, in freezer containers. To use, thaw and decorate as desired.

Servings—80 cookies

Next time you're in Twilight, drop by Caitlyn's flower shop, and she'll be happy to help you select flowers with cookie add-ons from the Twilight bakery. It makes a terrific holiday gift for the hostess in your life.

CHOCOLATE TOFFEE COOKIE SQUARES

Chocolate Toffee Cookie Squares

SUBMITTED BY SADIE COOL

*T*his lip-smacking good recipe comes from children's book author Sadie Cool, who...*nudge, nudge, wink, wink*...happens to be the pen name of Sarah Collier Walker. She and her daughter, Jazzy, invented this recipe when they were snowbound during the Christmas of 2015.

It's a personal favorite of her game warden hubby, Travis. (PS, *he* was the one Sadie/Sarah dreamed about when she put Kismet cookies under her pillow on Christmas Eve.)

INGREDIENTS

- 1/2 cup butter, cubed
- 32 caramels, unwrapped
- 1 can (14 ounces) sweetened condensed milk
- 1 package (18.25 ounces) yellow cake mix
- 1/2 cup vegetable oil
- 2 eggs
- 2 cups semisweet chocolate chips
- 1 Heath candy bar (1.4 ounces), chopped

Instructions

Sadie reminds you to preheat your oven to 350°. Lightly grease a 13x9-inch baking pan and set aside.

In a large saucepan, over medium-low heat, stir together the butter, caramels, and sweetened condensed milk until smooth. Remove from heat and allow to cool.

In a large mixing bowl with an electric mixer on medium speed, beat the cake mix, oil, and eggs until combined.

Stir in the chocolate and white chips and chopped Heath bar. The dough should stiffen.

Spread about 3/4 of the dough into the prepared pan.

Bake for 15 minutes then set on wire rack to cool for 10 minutes.

Pour caramel mixture over the crust. (You don't have to use the entire amount!)

Using rounded spoonfuls, drop remaining dough over caramel layer.

Return pan to oven and bake for 25 to 30 more minutes, or until edges are golden.

Cool pan on wire rack for 10 minutes then separate the bars from the pan by running a knife around outer edges.

Allow to cool an additional 40 minutes longer and then cover and refrigerate pan for at least one hour. (Sadie says this is the hardest part because the kids keep trying to sneak bites.)

Cut squares into desired size and shape.

Servings—16 cookies

Sadie likes to serve these beauties when she does book signings ate Ye Olde Book Nook on the Twilight town square. The kids go bananas for them.

SNICKERDOODLE SANDWICH COOKIES

Snickerdoodle Sandwich Cookies

Submitted by Carrie MacGregor

*C*arrie MacGregor submitted these bad boys, and they are seriously addictive. Yes, Carrie is Flynn's younger sister. The one who used to do all Flynn's knitting before Flynn came clean and admitted she didn't know how to knit.

Y'all, Carrie has some mad homemaking skills. Besides being an expert knitter, she's a pretty darn good baker. We all look forward to when Carrie comes back to town for the holidays with her husband, reality show host, Mark Leland.

Carrie says don't skip the extra step of the cinnamon caramel ganache. It makes these cookies the standouts that they are.

INGREDIENTS

For the cookies:
- 2 ½ cups all-purpose flour
- 2 teaspoons cream of tartar
- 1 teaspoon baking soda
- 3/4 teaspoon salt
- 1 ¾ cups granulated sugar, divided
- 1 cup (2 sticks) unsalted butter, softened
- 2 large eggs
- 1 tablespoon cinnamon

For the frosting:
- 2 sticks unsalted butter, softened
- 3 cups powdered sugar
- 1 ½ teaspoon ground cinnamon
- 2 to 3 teaspoons milk
- 3 teaspoons vanilla extract

For the cinnamon caramel ganache:
- 1 cup caramel baking bits
- 1/4 cup heavy cream
- 1 teaspoon ground cinnamon

. . .

Instructions

Carrie says for these cookies you need to kick the heat up a notch and preheat the oven to 400°. Then line several baking sheets with parchment paper. In a large bowl whisk together the flour, cream of tartar, baking soda, and salt. Set aside.

In the bowl of an electric mixer, cream butter and 1 ½ cups granulated sugar together until light and fluffy, about 3 to 5 minutes. Then beat in eggs and scrape the bowl. Turn mixer on low and slowly add flour mixture until well combined.

Mix the remaining 1/4 cup granulated sugar and cinnamon together in a small bowl. Use a teaspoon-sized cookie scoop to measure out dough balls. Roll each ball in your hands to even them out, then roll in cinnamon sugar to thoroughly coat.

Place the balls on prepared baking sheets, 2 ½ inches apart. Bake for 8 to 9 minutes, until just barely golden around the edges. Cool for several minutes on the baking sheets before moving.

For frosting, beat together butter and powdered sugar until well blended and smooth. Increase mixer speed and continue beating for another 3 minutes. Pour in vanilla extract and continue beating until combined. Add in ground cinnamon. Add 2 teaspoons milk and continue beating. If you feel the consistency is still too thick, add one more teaspoon of milk and beat again.

For the caramel cinnamon ganache, place caramel chips and cream in a microwave-safe bowl. Heat in the microwave in 15-second intervals, stirring in between until the mixture is smooth. Stir in the ground cinnamon. Let cool to room temperature.

To assemble: Match up two cookies that are of equal size and shape. Turn the bottom cookies over. Use a piping bag (or zip-bag with the corner cut off) to pipe the filling onto the bottom cookie. Add a spoonful of ganache filling. Add the top cookie on each sandwich and press down.

Servings—16 cookies

These cookies are as rich as Bill Gates, so make sure you have a cup of hot coffee or cold milk nearby to wash them down with.

GOOEY CHOCOLATE CARAMEL NUT COOKIE BARS

Gooey Chocolate Caramel Nut Cookie Bars

BY CHRISTINE NOBLE

$\mathcal{W}$hen Christine Noble, owner of the Twilight Bakery submits a cookie, you know it's going to be out-of-this-world. Everyone clamors for her gooey chocolate caramel nut cookie bar. Consider making two batches because these won't last long.

Christine's four kids say these are the best cookie bars they've ever eaten.

Ingredients

- 1 package (18.25 ounces) devil's food cake mix
- 3/4 cup butter, melted
- 1/2 cup milk, divided
- 60 caramels, unwrapped
- 1 cup walnuts, coarsely chopped
- 1 cup semisweet chocolate chips
- 1 cup white chocolate chunks, chopped

Instructions

Preheat oven to 350°. Lightly grease a 13x9-inch baking pan and set aside.

In a medium bowl, combine cake mix, butter, and 1/4 cup milk and mix well.

Press half of the batter into the bottom of prepared pan and spread evenly.

Bake for 7 to 8 minutes or until batter just begins to form a crust—then remove from oven.

Meanwhile, combine caramels and remaining 1/4 cup milk in a heavy medium-size saucepan. Cook over low heat, stirring often, about 5 minutes or until caramels are melted, and the mixture is smooth. Pour melted caramel mixture over partially baked crust.

Combine walnuts, chocolate chips, and white chocolate chunks and sprinkle over caramel layer.

Drop spoonfuls of remaining batter evenly over nut and chocolate chip layer.

Return pan to oven and bake 18 to 20 minutes more, or until top layer springs back when lightly touched. (Caramel center will still be soft).

Cool pan on wire rack before cutting bars into desired size and shape. Cookie bars should be stored in airtight container. Of course, with four kids in the house, Christine doesn't have to worry about leftovers.

Servings—16 cookies

Bars may be frozen; let thaw 20 to 25 minutes before serving. Which makes these cookies perfect for last-minute entertaining.

PECAN AND CHOCOLATE CHIP BARS

PECAN CHOCOLATE CHIP BARS

Rules are Made to Be Broken

SUBMITTED BY RAYLENE PRINGLE

*Y*es, it's basically a chocolate cookie and therefore violates Rule #4 of Cookie Club rules.

But Raylene Pringle says she doesn't give a rat's patooty (except we all know she didn't say patooty). Rules were made to be broken, especially with these scrumptious cookies.

And we all know that no one in The First Love Cookie Club is about to toss Raylene out on her ear for a rule violation. After all, she was once a Dallas Cowboys cheerleader.

Plus, let's face facts, Raylene is the life of the party. Anyone who runs a bar called The Horny Toad Tavern can break any rules she wants.

INGREDIENTS
- 1 cup butter, softened
- 1 cup packed brown sugar
- 1 cup granulated sugar
- 2 eggs
- 1 tablespoon vanilla extract
- 2 cups flour
- 1 teaspoon baking soda
- 1/2 teaspoon salt
- 2 cups semisweet chocolate chips

Instructions
Preheat oven to 350°. Lightly grease a 13x9-inch baking pan and set aside.

Cream butter, brown sugar, and granulated sugar for 4 minutes, until light and fluffy. Stir in eggs and vanilla extract and mix well.

In another bowl, mix flour, baking soda, and salt. Stir in the flour mixture just until blended.

Stir in pecans and chocolate chips. Bake for 28 to 34 minutes, or until light golden brown. Let cool for 10 minutes before cutting into squares. Raylene recommends pairing these cookies with a red dessert wine or hearty port.

Servings—16 cookies

TEXAS SHEETCAKE COOKIES

LORI WILDE & CHRISTIE CONLEE

Texas Sheetcake Cookies

From the First Love Cookie Club

SUBMITTED BY SHANNON DEAVERS

*T*hese cake-style cookies have a place deep in the heart of Texans. The recipe was submitted by Shannon Deavers who is as sweet and refined as her biological mother, Raylene, is sassy, spicy, and well...um...somewhat less refined.

Shannon didn't find her true love, former Navy SEAL, Nate, until she tracked down her mother. Raylene had given her up for adoption when Shannon was a baby.

Now, mother and daughter are thick as thieves, and Shannon's romance with Nate is the stuff of kismet cookie legend.

Both Shannon and Nate are over forty, but they've got four kids—including a set of twins—that keep them young and on their toes.

INGREDIENTS

For the cookies:

1/2 cup unsalted butter (softened at room temperature)

1/3 cup granulated sugar

1 egg

1 teaspoon vanilla

1 teaspoon baking powder

1/2 teaspoon salt

1 ⅓ cup flour

1/2 cup semi-sweet chocolate chips (or 3.01 oz. semisweet baking chocolate) melted

For the Icing:

1/2 cup unsalted butter

2 tablespoon cocoa powder

3 tablespoon milk

1 teaspoon vanilla

2 ½ cups powdered sugar

. . .

Instructions

Preheat oven to 350° Line baking sheet with parchment paper and set aside. Beat butter and sugar until light and fluffy.

Add in egg and vanilla and mix until well combined, mix in salt and baking powder.

Gradually add in flour while mixing on low speed (dough should be thick).

Mix in melted chocolate.

Drop about a tablespoon size mound of dough onto baking sheet.

Bake about 8 minutes (do not overbake, the cookies should just appear set, but to stay soft on the inside).

Transfer to a wire rack to cool.

For the icing:

Combine butter, cocoa powder, milk, and vanilla in a medium saucepan over medium heat, whisk until melted and combine, take from the heat and whisk in powdered sugar, pour over the cookies and cool completely.

Servings—24 cookies

Best when served the same day they're baked.

Oh, Shannon has a bit of news to share. Baby #5 is due on Christmas Day.

ABOUT THE AUTHOR

Lori Wilde is the *New York Times, USA* Today and Publishers' Weekly bestselling author of 85 works of romantic fiction. She's a three time Romance Writers' of America RITA finalist and has four times been nominated for Romantic Times Readers' Choice Award.

She has won numerous other awards as well. Her books have been translated into 26 languages, with more than four million copies of her books sold worldwide. Her breakout novel, *The First Love Cookie Club,* has been optioned for a TV movie.

Lori is a registered nurse with a BSN from Texas Christian University. She holds a certificate in forensics, and is also a certified yoga instructor.

A fifth generation Texan, Lori lives with her husband, Bill, in the Cutting Horse Capital of the World; where they run Epiphany

Orchards, a writing/creativity retreat for the care and enrichment of the artistic soul.

facebook.com/LoriWildeBooks

twitter.com/loriwilde

bookbub.com/profile/lori-wilde

instagram.com/loriwilde02

pinterest.com/loriwilde

amazon.com/author/loriwilde

ABOUT THE BAKER

Christie Conlee is our intrepid baker who spent hours baking and taste-testing each recipe. This cookbook would not have been possible without her.

Made in the USA
Las Vegas, NV
27 August 2021